This book belongs to

_____

_____

_____

_____

Notes for grown-ups

This book practises:

- **Deeper Understanding:** Concentrating on a single subject allows for deeper exploration and understanding without being overwhelmed by distractions from multiple tasks and topics.
- **Improved Retention:** When children focus solely on one subject, they are more likely to retain information. This concentrated learning helps solidify concepts in their memory.
- **Enhanced Skill Development:** Mastering one skill at a time encourages kids to develop proficiency and expertise. This focused practice can lead to greater confidence and competence in the area they are learning.
- **Reduced Anxiety:** Juggling multiple subjects or activities can create stress and anxiety. Focusing on one thing can simplify a child's learning experience and reduce feelings of being overwhelmed.
- **Stronger Connections:** Learning one thing deeply can help children make connections between concepts and ideas, enhancing their ability to apply knowledge in practical situations.
- **Personalized Learning:** Concentrating on one subject provides opportunities for personalized learning, allowing children to move at their own pace and adapt their studies to their interests and strengths.

With a love for storytelling and a commitment to empowering the next generation, we have developed this activity book to encourage exploration, discovery, and joy in learning. We believe that every child has the potential to learn and grow when provided with the right tools and opportunities. Through this book, we hope to spark curiosity and encourage children to embrace the wonderful journey of knowledge and creativity.

First published 2024

© Olena Spektor

Learning Number

1

START

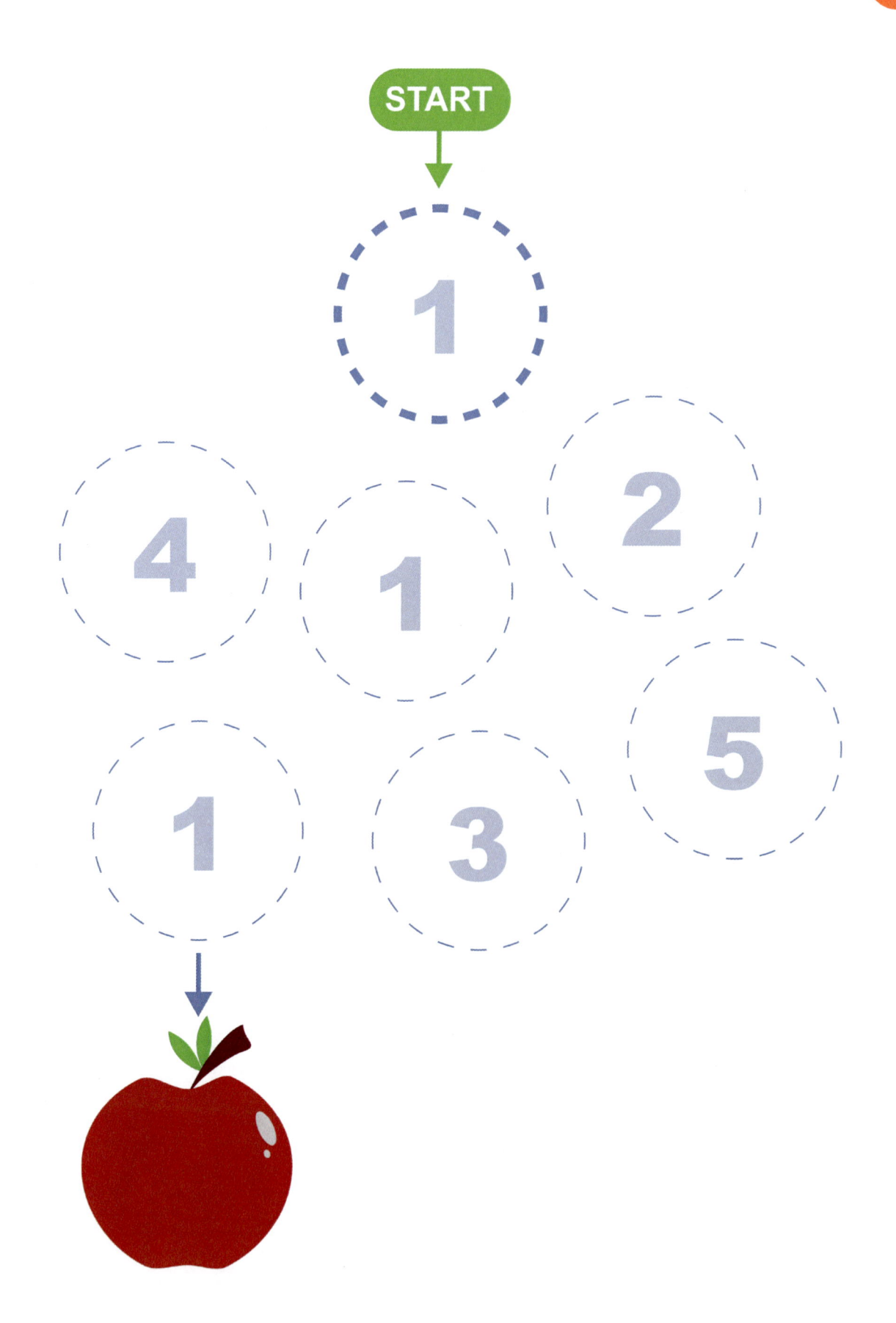

1

4　1　2

1　3　5

START

START

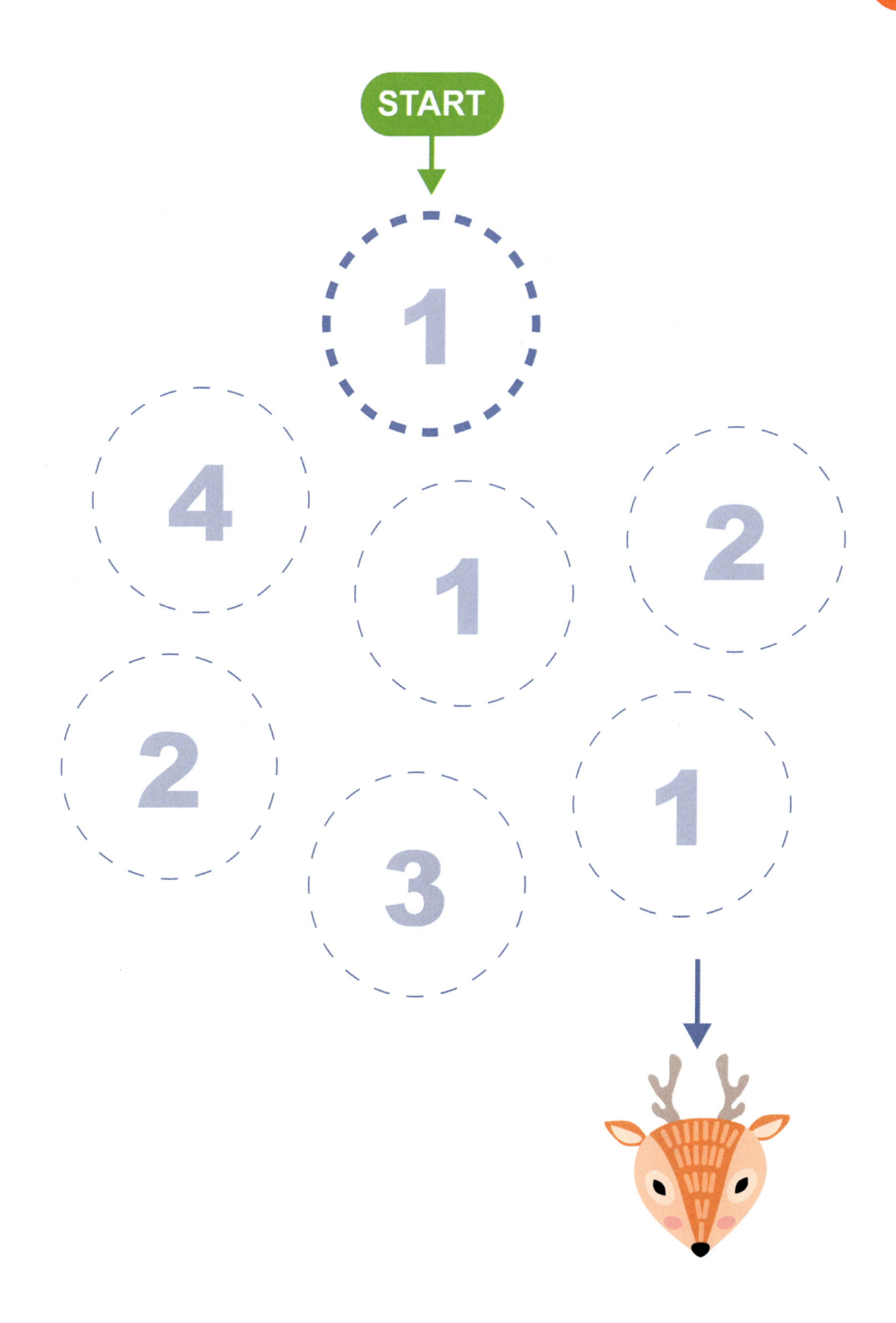

1

4
1
2

2
1
3

4

START

	1	2
1	3	4
2	1	1	5
3	4	1

START

1 1
 5 3 1
2 8 1 5
 3 4 1

START

1　1

1　3　1

1　8　4　5

1　1　1

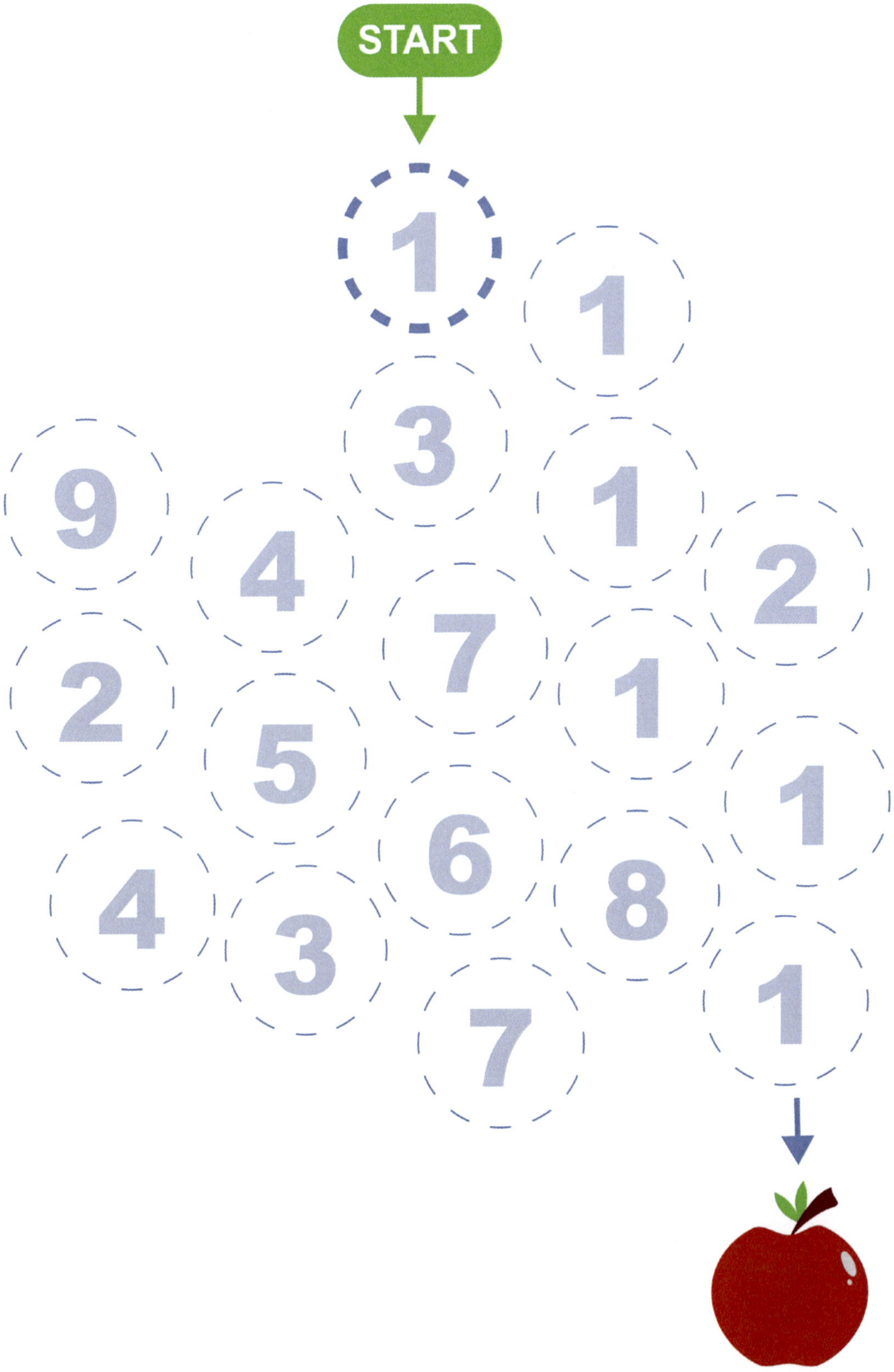
START

8

START

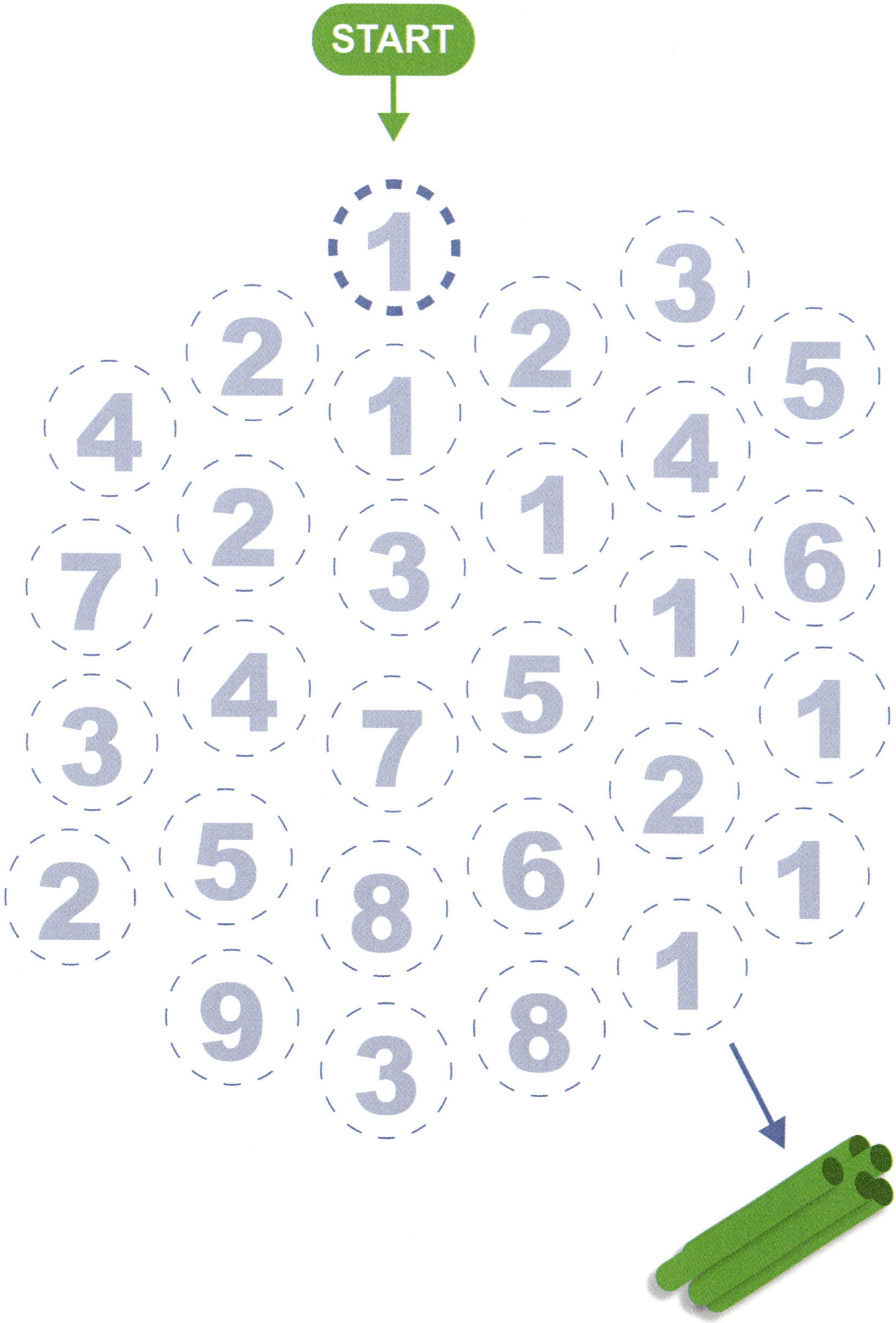
START

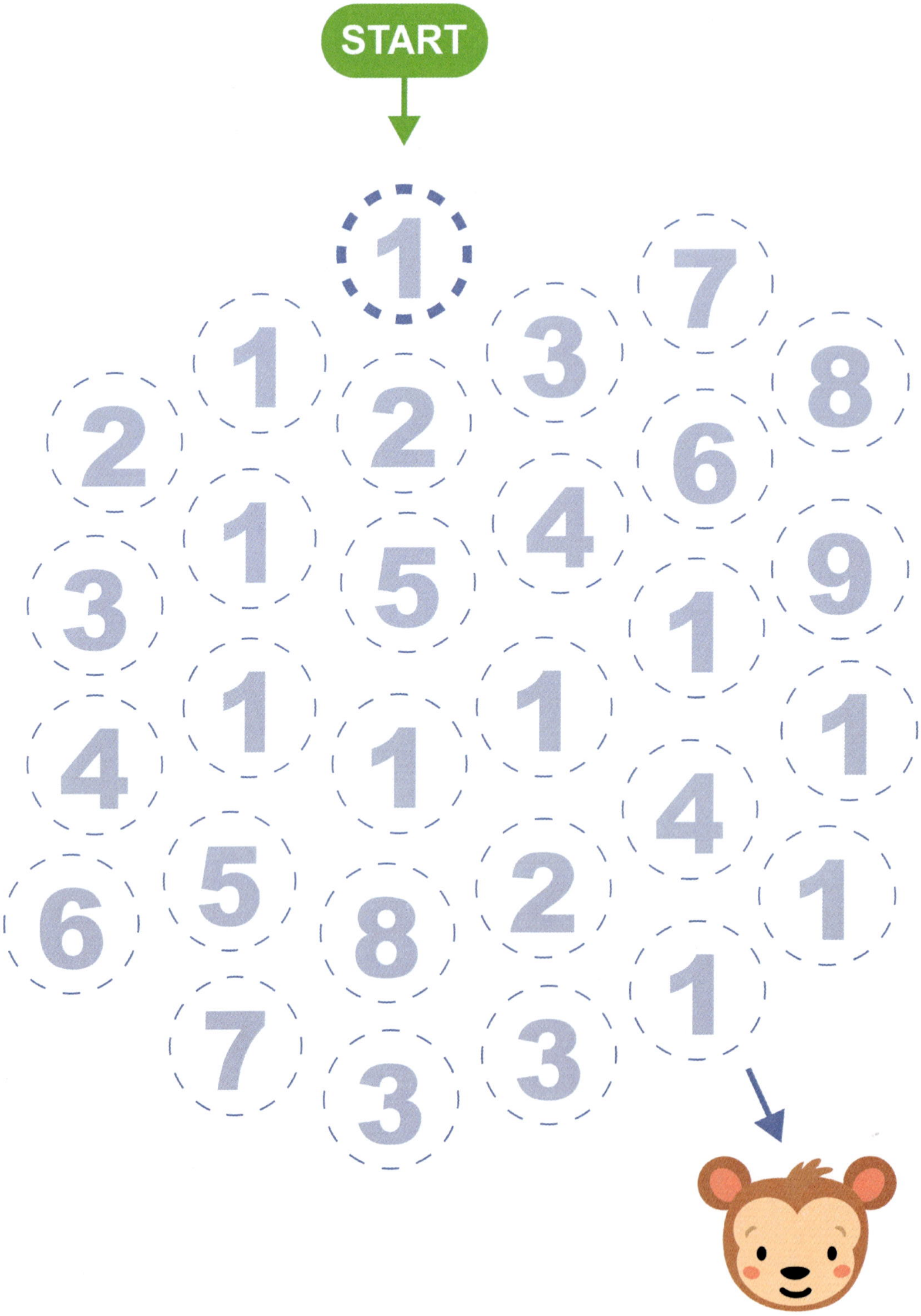
START

START

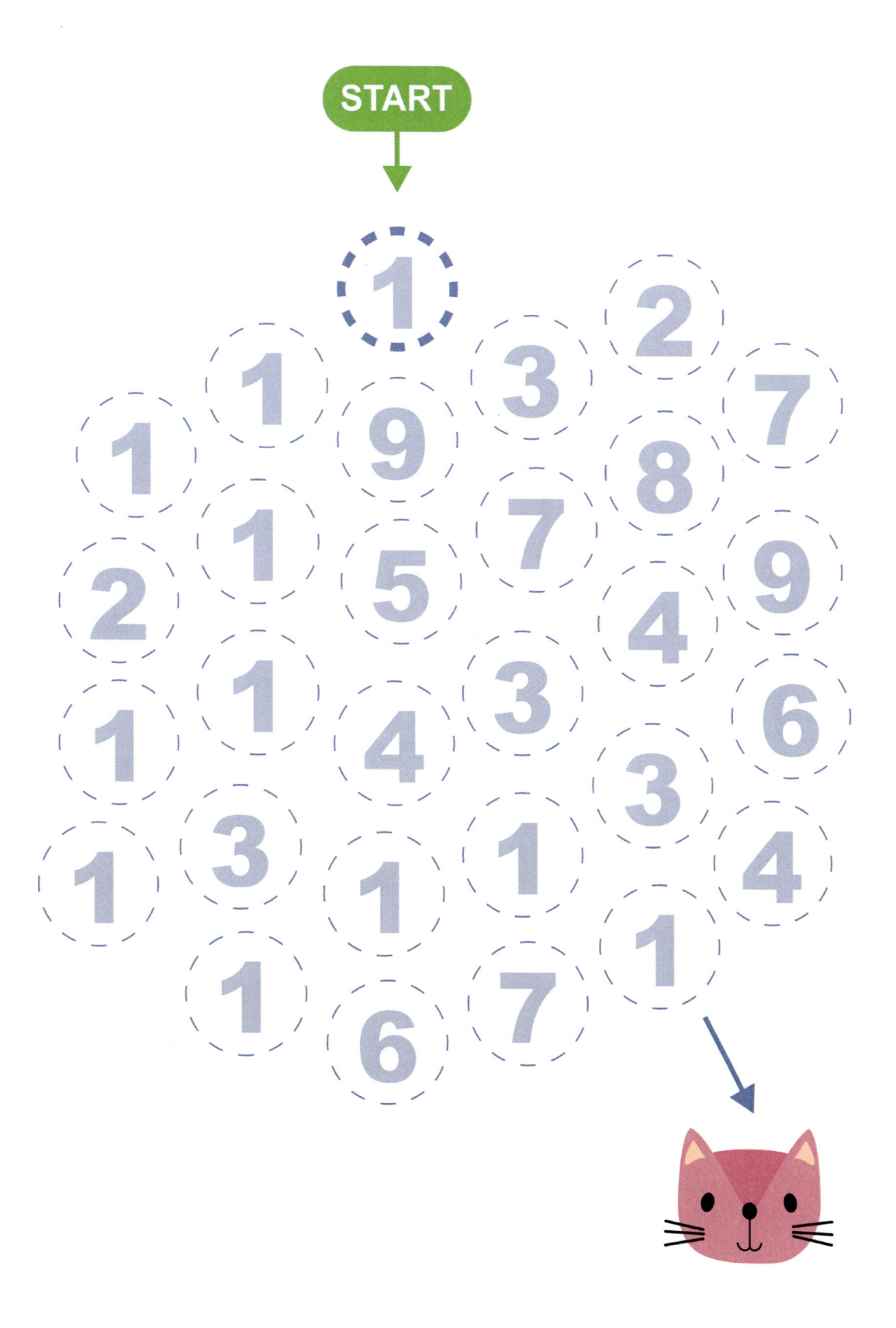

12

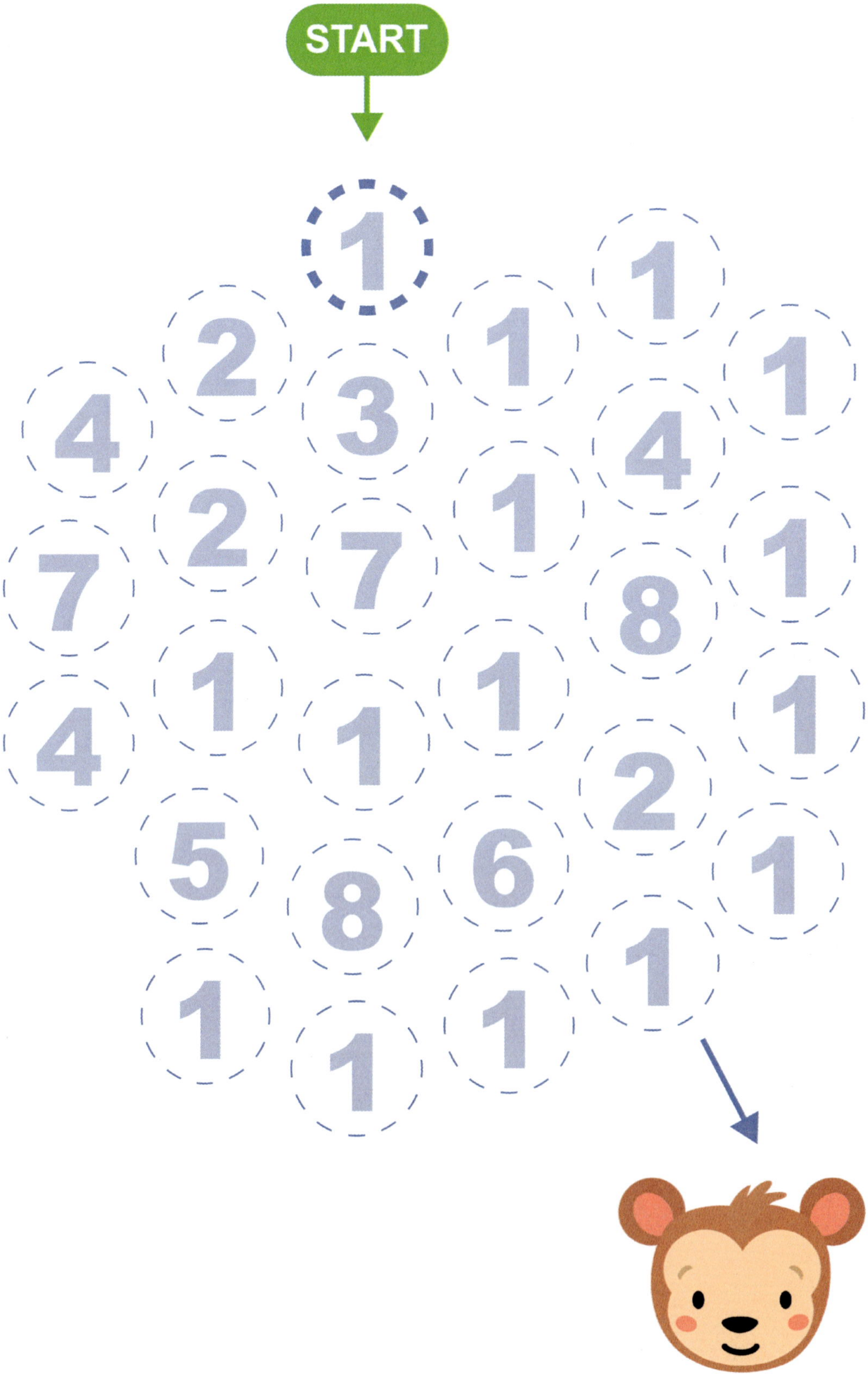
START

14

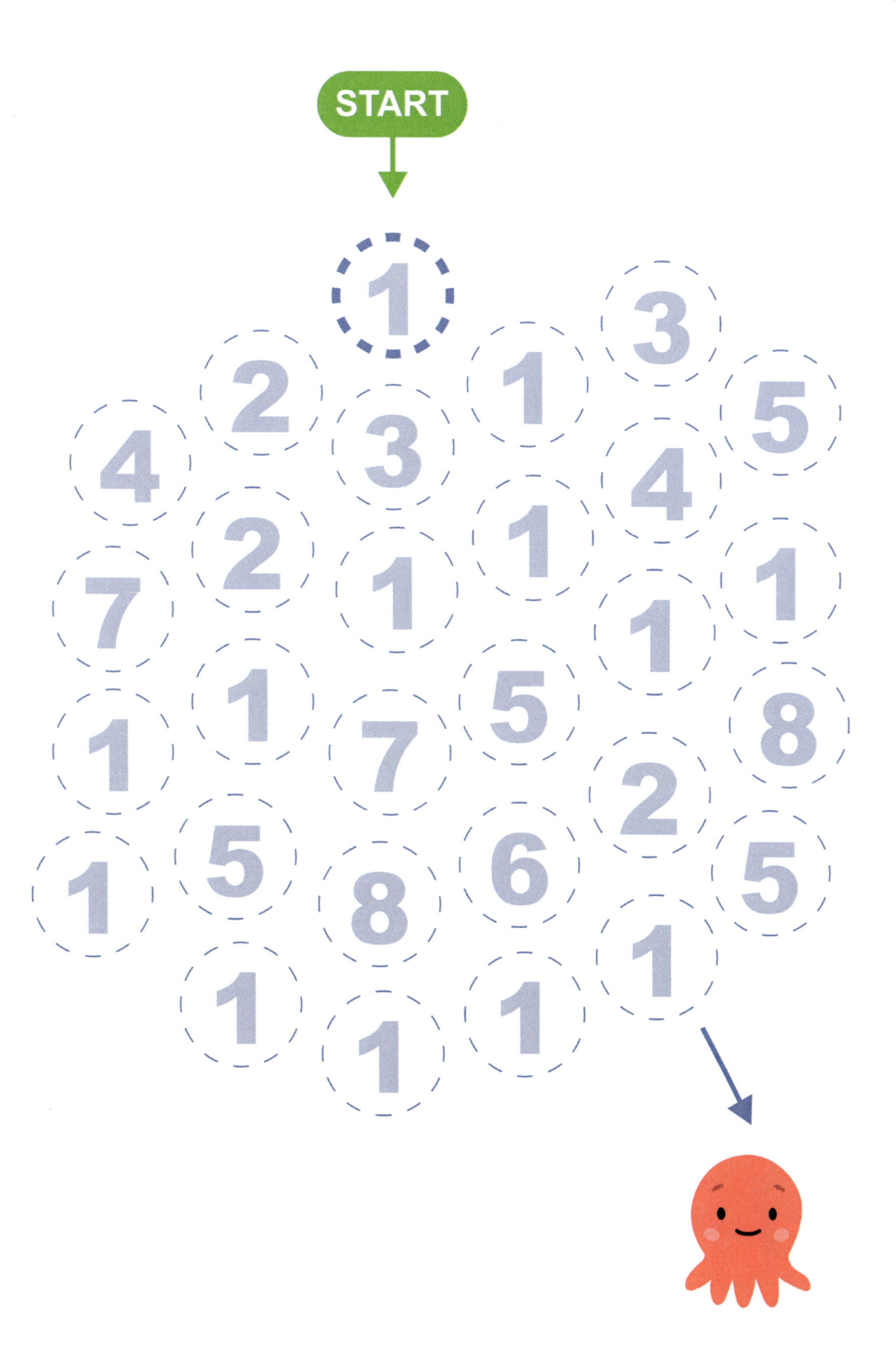

15

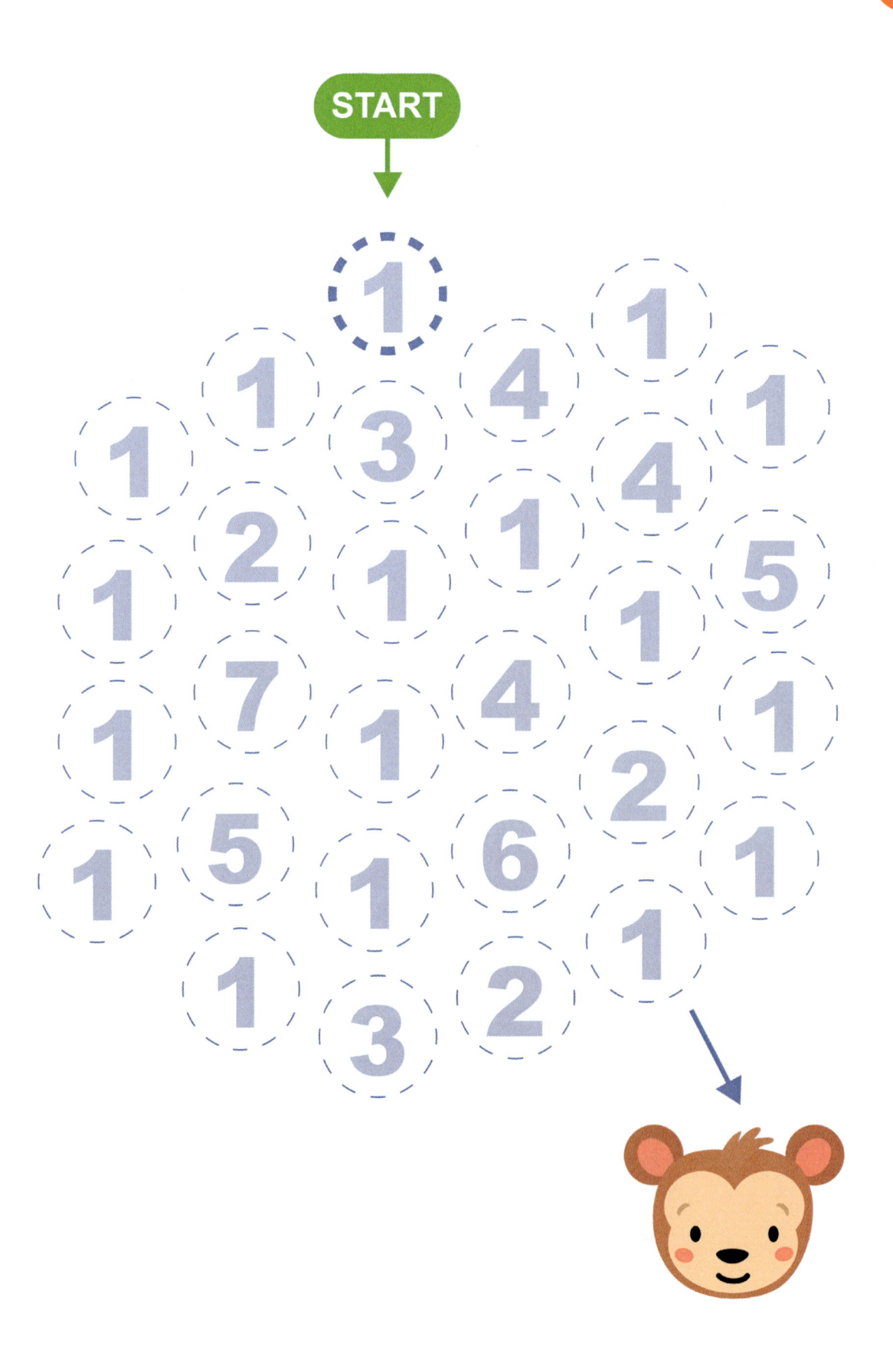

START

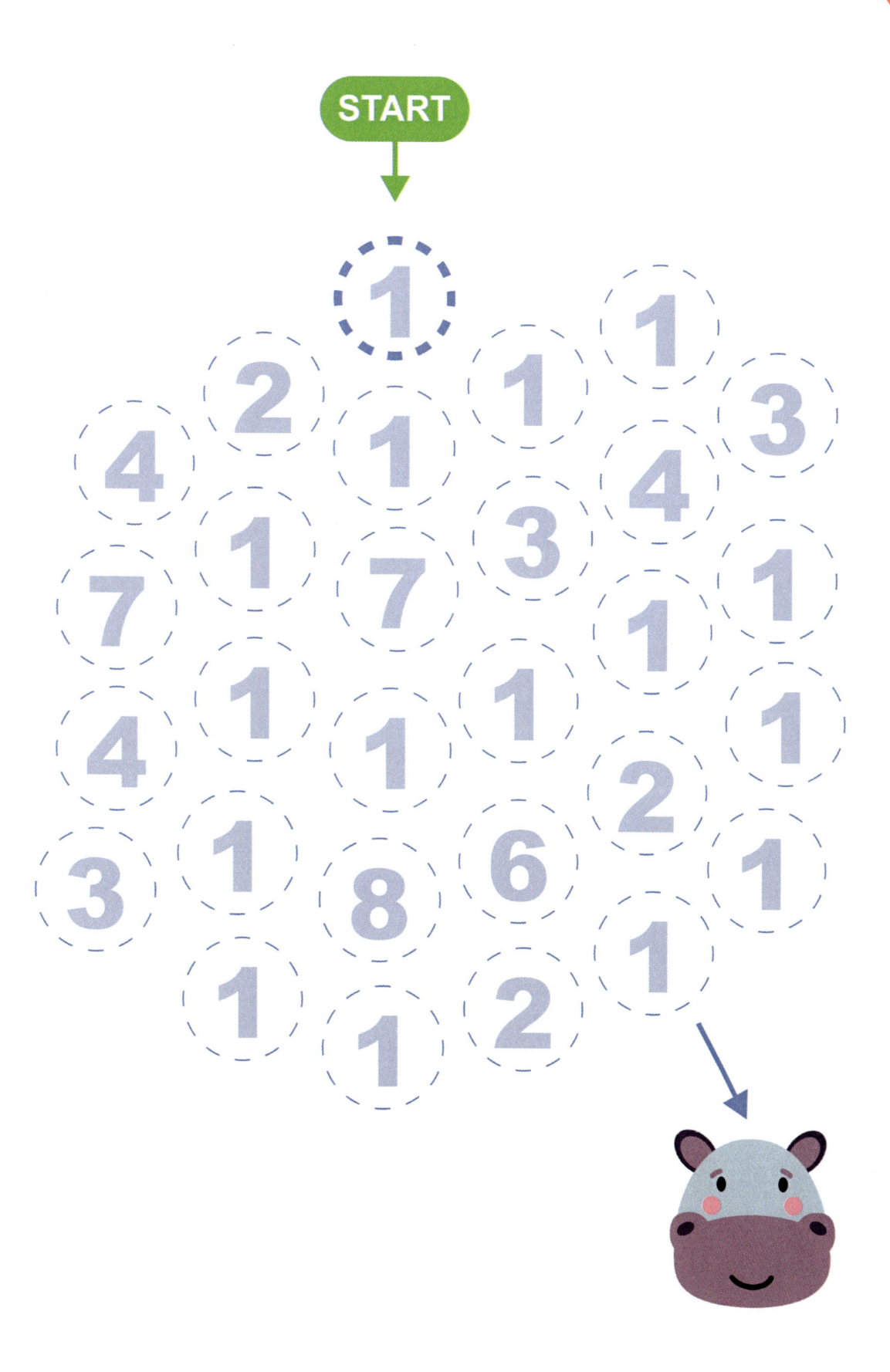

16

START

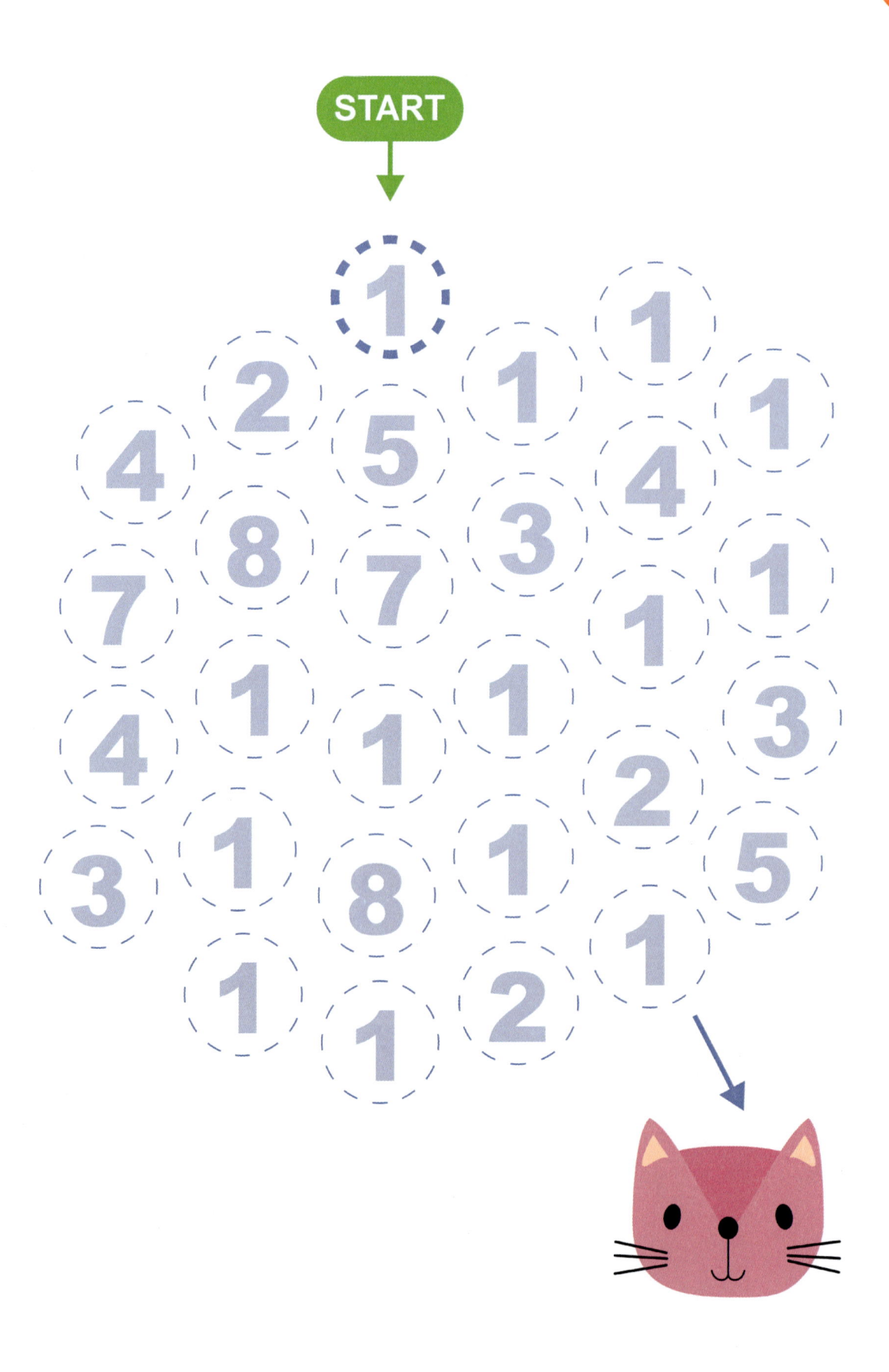

START

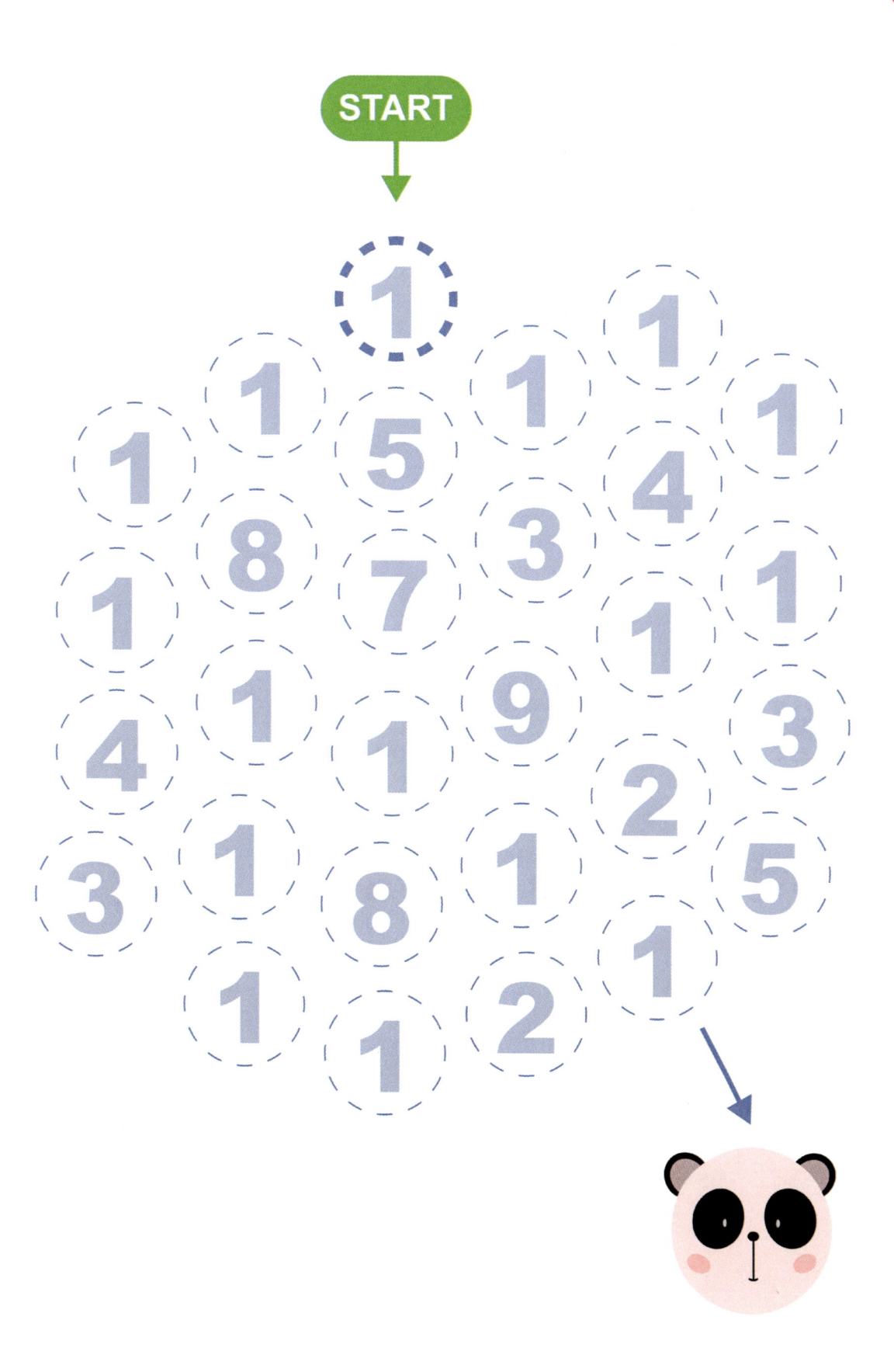

18

Trace the number

1 1 1 1 1 1

1 1 1 1 1 1

1 1 1 1 1 1

1 1 1 1 1 1

1 1 1 1 1 1

Answers

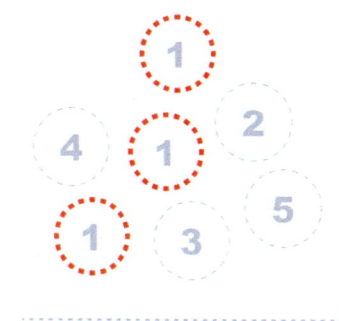

1
2
3
4
5
6
7
8
9

10

11

12

13

14

15

16

17

18

Made in the USA
Las Vegas, NV
24 June 2025